Nigel's Choice

Rai White

Nigel's Choice

A Novel by Rai White

More Books by Rai White

- ❖ Before And After I Do

- ❖ Real Love Is….

- ❖ Real Love Is….2: The 25th Year

- ❖ From Rags To Stitches

- ❖ Japheth Can Count

Nigel's Choice

Published by Raynell White

Copyright © 2016 Raynell White

Cover model **Sherard Amiger**

Graphic Designer **Glenn Davis**

Printed in United States Of America

ISBN-10   1015344929762

ISBN-13   978-1534929760

Acknowledgements

I'd like to give a special thanks to my cover model, Mr. Sherard Amiger, for being a model a second time on one of my books. The life of a writer is late nights, long hours, when they're working on a new piece. Even the shortest books can take some time. However, when an author is done, and he or she sees their completed project, they feel so elated…like it's been worth it all.

Thanks to everyone that has encouraged me to keep moving forth in faith, with my writing, especially, during challenging times. You know who you are. I've learned to look to God in all areas of my life, trusting that he'll bless whatever I put forth my hands to do. Also, thanks to all of you that have bought copies of my paperbacks and kindle books, and to those of you who've taken the time to read my work, I truly appreciate it; it means a lot to me. God bless you all.

TABLE OF CONTENTS

PREFACE

Are you experiencing deep emotional pain that won't go away because of mistreatment in various forms, and/or ridicule and bullying, that has been continuously done to you by certain individuals? Do you find yourself feeling bitter whenever you think about it? Are you holding unforgiveness in your heart against them-you want to forgive them, but you just honestly, don't know how?

Then, this book "Nigel's Choice" will be a good read for you. Nigel was 6 foot 3, handsome, light skinned, with a slender muscular build. He served two terms in the Marine Corps before being honorably discharged and using his Master's Degree, to obtain a position in a major corporation, in downtown Chicago. His colleagues looked up to him. He was a hardworking, positive person, who never had anything negative to say about anyone. His female colleagues adored him because of his personality and good looks. His family and others close to him saw him as a go-getter, living the good life.

Nigel would agree to that. However, even though life was good, he had an issue that was preventing his life from being even better. Then, one day he made the choice to reach out and get the help he needed.

The main emphasis of this book is for people to learn how to forgive. That doesn't mean that those individuals won't have some scars left from the emotional trauma that they've suffered.

For example, when people get deep physical wounds and extreme injuries, there are usually visible scars left on a person's body even after they've healed. I was conversing with someone who'd been in a motorcycle accident, and he was explaining to me about the visible scars on his body. That area on his body had healed. However, he said that it actually healed too fast on the outside. It had healed on the outside first, leaving areas of dark, shiny scars on his body. Therefore, sometimes, there will be scars left in the lives of people who've been hurt emotionally, even though they've forgiven the individuals who caused their pain. So, they may need your patience and compassion. So, be kind....

CHAPTER ONE
The Good Life

Just as handsome as ever, Nigel Austella, had maintained his slender build that he'd had since childhood (which he inherited from his father), except now, he no longer appeared frail. Obviously, he had developed his fine looking physique that he now had, while serving time in the Marine Corps. Nigel had served two terms in the Marine Corps-one which consisted of a tour of duty in Iraq. He served his country well and returned back home to Chicago, Illinois, with an honorable discharge, as well as a Master's Degree in Public Administration. He applied and was hired at a major corporation, in Chicago.

Nigel excelled quickly within the corporation. He'd really made a name for himself, among his colleagues who greatly admired him. It seemed as though everyone loved Nigel. He was an awesome guy, with a great personality. He was very positive, and he had nothing negative to say about anyone. Women adored him. They loved his light skinned complexion-his gorgeous skin that appeared as though he'd never aged.

They teased him sometimes and referred to him as "baby face" because of that. One of his female co-workers sang to him, "baby face, you've got the cutest little baby face." She chuckled and winked her eye at him as she walked off-heading back to her office after a conference they had that particular day.

Nigel grew up in Chicago, but his family was originally from Atlanta, Georgia. He spent many summers in Atlanta, visiting with relatives; and he was a fan of anything associated with Atlanta-the "**A**", as he referred to it. He was a fan of everything from their sports' teams to their southern, soul food. He even loved their fresh peaches-the fruit, that is. He has been known to date a few, sweet, country reared, southern ladies from Georgia-also known as "Georgia Peaches".

Nigel's family and others who knew him personally looked up to him. They saw him as a go-getter. All they could see was that Nigel was living **the good life**. Nigel, himself, would agree. However, that was excluding one secret that he'd been hiding for years. It had started to

really bother him, though. He knew he had
to vent to someone; he just wasn't sure
who to trust enough to talk to, in such a
way. One night after a long day's work,
Nigel decided to stop at his favorite
restaurant and bar, downtown. He hadn't
eaten anything at all, except for a palm full
of peanuts. He loved that particular
restaurant's grilled beef tenderloin roast
with carrots and fennel; and they made
pina coladas that were out of this world.
However, Nigel always ordered virgin
drinks.

While sitting at the bar, Nigel noticed a
guy that walked into the restaurant; he had
a look of distress on his face. The man
headed to the bar. Nigel made eye contact
and spoke to him. The man also spoke, as
he took a seat at the bar. Nigel thought to
himself, that the poor fellow was about to
try and drink his pain away. As soon as he
finished his thought, the man ordered a
virgin pina colada, as well. The bartender
commented, "seems as though a lot of our
customers are on this virgin thing, tonight.
Ha, ha, ha!" The man replied, "I don't
drink anymore."

CHAPTER TWO
Challenging Times

The man turned and looked at Nigel. "Even when I'm facing **challenging times**, I learned a long time ago, that alcohol only makes it worse. I used to try and drink away the pain when I would have issues going on; and I became an alcoholic. It ruined my life. I lost everything I had-my car, my house, and the furniture in it. My wife and I had just gotten up on our feet. We worked hard for what we had, to just lose it like that.

It was my fault; I hate that I caused my family to suffer like that. It takes a good woman to stay with you during times like that, especially when you're the one that caused all the unnecessary problems." He shook his head. "I'll tell you one thing, I started to just end it all, but I couldn't do it because of the way I was raised. I knew it would be wrong for me to take my own life.

I started getting DUI's, which eventually led to my license being suspended. Unfortunately, we had a car, and I could no longer drive it to get to work. So, I had to be dropped off to work, or catch public transportation. After a while, I started being late for work because I'd overslept. My wife was busy getting ready for work, herself. She'd try to wake me up, but she couldn't stay there and watch me get ready. By the time I'd get ready and she'd drop me off, I'd be late for work. I got by with that for a while, but it eventually led to me getting fired. After that, my wife's income alone, was not enough to pay all the bills. So, our car got repossessed. My wife was at work one day, and when she got ready to leave, she didn't see our car anywhere in the parking lot. She couldn't find it anywhere.

Security was about to help her search for it, but when the officer asked what type of car it was and she told him, he knew where it was. He told her, 'ma'am, I saw a guy from a repo company put your car on a tow truck and he drove away with it. I'm so sorry.'" "My wife was so embarrassed. Then, the furniture company repossessed our furniture and the bank foreclosed on our beautiful, home." The man took a deep sigh.

"I'll tell you another thing, too; I had never cried out to God like I did after all those things happened. Man, he heard my cry and he changed my life. We were living with my wife's sister and her husband. Then, God blessed us to relocate into a nice apartment, where we now live with our baby girl. We're still walking and using public transportation to get around, right now, but all of that is about to change. God is not through blessing us, yet. Oh, I must mention that he blessed me with another job. My wife still has the same job; she's been there several years, now. She's gotten a few raises, too. I give God all the glory."

Nigel looked at the guy and shook his head-mumbling to himself, "wow, and I thought I had problems!" Nigel didn't take his own situation lightly. He knew he definitely needed God to do something in his life. He was just counting his blessings, after hearing all the stuff the man said that he'd gone through.

The man paused for a couple of seconds, then, resumed the discussion about his daughter. "Bruh, after all I've been through already, I kept hope when there was no hope left in me, if that makes any sense to you." The man paused again. "After all the other stuff that's already happened, then, I got word about some stuff that happened to my baby girl." The man shook his head. Nigel said, "wow, man; be strong, my brother. By the way, what is your name, bruh?" "Oh, I'm sorry, man. I came in here and just started dropping my troubles on you…didn't even introduce myself." "It's alright, man; it's completely alright. By the way, I'm Nigel." "Yeah, okay, my name is Mitchell, man. I found out that one of the neighbors had been messing with my daughter. Well, he's a former neighbor, now. He hit it big in the stock market, during a time when it was booming; and he's moved into a big, nice home, somewhere near this area.

Bruh, this is exactly how my baby girl, Lucy, said that everything went down- from the first day he hurt my baby. She was outside playing in her Easter outfit and she was excited about the fact that we were having an Easter egg hunt right after church service. She was talking to some of the other kids about the Easter egg hunt.

One of the kids said, 'aww, shut up, Lucy!
You just think you look good in your
Easter outfit. I have a new outfit too. My
whole family, have new outfits for
Easter.'" "Lucy responded back, 'Sally,
you are just sooo mean, all the time.'"
"As Lucy was telling the other kids about
the Easter egg hunt, my wife, Cheryl
called her inside. Cheryl didn't want her to
get her outfit dirty.

The way our apartment building is
structured, Lucy had to go inside of a
hallway in our building to get to our
apartment door. There was an apartment
right next to ours on the opposite side. My
wife was upstairs in one of the bedrooms
when she called down to her to come
inside. As Lucy went inside to head to our
apartment, a neighbor, Bob, whose
apartment was next door on the opposite
side, stepped outside of his apartment door
and grabbed Lucy. He covered her mouth
with his hand. He picked her up and took
her inside into his bedroom. She said that
he had the curtains in the bedroom pulled
opened; and as he carried her pass the
window, she focused her eyes on the
beautiful multi-colored leaves on the tree,

outside. He laid her on his bed and quickly raped her. He told her that she'd better not tell anyone; and then he told her to hurry home before her mom got upset.

Bob had heard my wife call down to Lucy, to come inside right after he'd finished watching some porn. He told Lucy that he'd been looking at some grown folks' movies, and that he waited for her to come inside of the building. Lucy said that he even told her that he was sorry for what he did, but he had a porn addiction. If you've got an addiction like that, you get help! You don't rape innocent, kids!" Mitchell paused and shook his head.

"Anyhow, Lucy went home. She said that she let her mom know she was there. Then, she nervously headed straight to the bathroom. She felt so nasty. She took off her clothes and got back into the tub and took a second bath. She scrubbed and scrubbed to try and get rid of the disgusting feeling that she felt. She noticed some blood on her also, and she washed all of that away. After that, she took a bottle of perfume and sprayed her thighs excessively. She came out of the bathroom and went into her bedroom, and her mom asked if she was ready. She told me she said, 'yes, ma'am.'" "Her mom told her to come on, so we'd not be late for the church service. As soon as Lucy got near her mom, Cheryl said to her, 'whew, Lucy, you smell like you're wearing the whole bottle of perfume.'"

"Lucy said that she didn't respond to her mom's comment; she was afraid and ashamed to tell her mom and myself what Bob had done to her. She was afraid of what Bob might do. Lucy, Cheryl, and I, left for church.

I noticed Bob as he peeped out of his window-watching us as we left our apartment complex. The church was in walking distance of the apartments. After that day, Lucy became reserved. We noticed it, and we were concerned. However, we didn't think it was anything too serious-just that it was perhaps a part of growing up.

Lucy said that there were several other times that Bob stopped her, on her way to our apartment, and told her to come inside of his apartment. She voluntarily went inside of his apartment each of those times, and he'd rape her and tell her she'd better not say anything about it to anyone. Lucy would do just as he said to do. She said that she'd begun to feel numb to the things he was doing to her. Then, as she continued to grow up, she became more reserved and rebellious towards Cheryl and me. We definitely noticed the change in her. However, we really became concerned at that time because this wasn't the Lucy that we knew. Whenever we'd inquire about the reason for her behavior, she'd say that she was okay. We knew she wasn't okay.

One day, Cheryl and I were relaxing and watching a talk show, when we saw a kid on there who was telling her story. Her behavior had changed just as Lucy's had. As the teen told more of her story, she eventually got to the part where she revealed that the change in behavior was due to sexual abuse. Cheryl and I immediately, looked at each other. We both were thinking the same thing (that perhaps this had happened to our little girl), but who-who would've done this to our little girl?

14

At that time, Lucy had just turned 13 and was preparing to start her last year of middle school in a few weeks. We certainly wanted to find out if this had happened to her before she entered her last year of middle school.

So, one day, I told my wife that we had to get to the bottom of things, and that perhaps she'd been molested like the other girl we saw on television. We both agreed, and we went upstairs and knocked on Lucy's bedroom door. She opened her door. We asked if we could sit down and have a talk with her. She said, 'sure you can.'" "I just came right out and asked Lucy if she'd ever been sexually abused. She said, 'no.'"

"Then, as my wife started to discuss how her behavior had changed, she immediately noticed blood on one of Lucy's arms. So, Cheryl asked, 'why is there blood on your arm?!'" 'Oh, it's nothing-just a paper cut, mom.'" "That's what Lucy said, while carefully, keeping her forearm turned downward, attempting to conceal the cuts on her wrist. My wife and I paused a second before we continued our interrogation. Our baby girl just burst into tears. That's when she opened up and told us what happened to ruin her life and change her behavior. She told us all that Bob had done to her-even how he'd made threats to her if she told anyone. She explained how that what he'd done to her had led her to start cutting herself on her wrist, with razor blades. She said, 'the first time that he raped me and I left his apartment, I felt so nasty; and I felt even nastier after seeing blood on my body. Then, I knew I had to find some type of therapy to help me get pass that.

So, a while after that, I started cutting myself. I didn't start doing it immediately. Eventually, it just crossed my mind one day, to cut myself and get relief. I know it may sound crazy, but once I started to do that, it brought back memories of the blood on my body, on that day, in particular. However, I felt relieved to see blood flowing out of me. It gave me a feeling of being cleansed of the sexual abuse and the pain of the whole situation…cleansed, period. So, I continued to do it again and again. I hate what that monster did to me!'"

"When she told us who had done those things to her, we remembered Bob quite well. However, we've kept it a secret for quite a while…too long. We tried to work it out among our family. We did that for Lucy's sake, but it's not working. Things have gone from bad to worse. So, I knew I had to find Bob and resolve this issue by whatever means I find necessary. I heard that he's living pretty well off of the returns from his investments.

I inquired and got some information about where he hung out from some of the guys in our neighborhood, who still speak with him, at times. Some of the fellows he used to hang out with told me that he likes to come here for the drinks. That's why I'm here, tonight, bruh. I thought I'd hang out here for a while, and see if he'll come in…heard he's a regular at the bar."

Mitchell, unconsciously, started slowly, beating his right fist into his left palm, and appeared to be in deep thought. He then, suddenly, looked back over at Nigel. "Man, my baby girl told me all he did to her, and I wanted to cry. Another part of me wants to kill him, but I know I must forgive him, if I want God to forgive my

sins. I know it's a lot, but bruh, I need to
vent. I just need to talk to somebody."
Nigel said, "bruh, just let it out; I'm
listening, man. I can feel your pain."

Mitchell had changed over the years.
He'd put on some weight and muscles,
through working out. Bob still looked
thick and carried his weight well.
However, Mitchell didn't notice right
away, but Bob had come inside and
sat at the bar, next to Nigel. Bob didn't
recognize Mitchell, but he overheard him
venting. He only heard the last statement
that Mitchell said to Nigel, who was
sitting between the both of them. "Yeah,
man, he raped our baby girl like that."

Bob quickly got into the conversation
and began to comment on what Mitchell
had said. Mitchell looked around at him.
He immediately recognized him as soon as
Bob said, "if that was my daughter, I'd
find that man and kill him!" In a rage,
Mitchell said, "you're doing all of this
talking, and you are that man! I ought to
kill you, pervert! I ought to kill you for the
things that you did to my baby girl!"

Bob said, "hold-hold; wait a minute, now! Whatcha talking about, man?" "You don't remember me, do you, Bob?!" By the puzzled look on Bob's face, it was obvious he didn't recognize Mitchell. "Yeah, I know you don't, but I remember you…sitting over there running your mouth. You sounded like David in the bible, talking about how you'd kill a man if he did something like that to your daughter. Well, you are that man, bruh! Thou art the man!" By this time, the bartender had become aware of what was going on. So, he and Nigel quickly, got in between the two. They tried to calm Mitchell so he wouldn't get in trouble.

The bartender called the police and told them what was taking place. Once they arrived, Mitchell told them his story. Bob denied it all. An officer called Mitchell aside and gave him some information so that he and his family could file charges, if they desired. He advised him that the proper way to handle a situation such as that was to file charges, and then, they'd conduct an investigation. Bob rushed out of the restaurant and bar, while Mitchell was conversing with the officer. Mitchell listened carefully to all that the officer had to say. Then, he thanked the officer, left the bar and went home. He told Cheryl about the incident and the information the officer had given to him. They spoke with a lawyer the next day so that they could file charges against Bob. The authorities said that because of the time that had gone by since the situation happened, unfortunately, the statute of limitations had run out.

However, they told Mitchell and Cheryl that if Bob did it back then, there was a chance that he had done it, again. So, the authorities set up an undercover sting operation to try and catch Bob. The undercover authorities noticed that Bob was often going and coming, with a lot of young people, to and from his home. One day, their surveillance spotted him taking inappropriate pictures of some underage, young people, at his home. That was enough evidence to prove that he was involved in porn.

The police quickly moved in and arrested him. They got a search warrant and searched his home, computers, and everything they could think of that could be used as evidence, against him.

CHAPTER THREE
Self Affliction

When they first spoke with their pastor about their situation, Mitchell said, "Pastor Dove, Lucy was raped by a neighbor, when she was 11. We found out a few weeks before she entered the 8th grade. Authorities found pornographic material of children on Bob's computers. They found cameras in his home with inappropriate pictures of kids on them, as well. The police had enough evidence to hold Bob in jail without bond.

They held him until the time for his trial. Bob's trial didn't begin immediately. He sat in jail for at least a year before his trial started. During the time, Mitchell and Cheryl spent time getting help for their family. They got counseling from their pastor, Pastor Dove. In addition to being a spiritual leader, he also had a Master's degree in Psychology.

We knew she'd become withdrawn; and as she got older, she became more withdrawn and rebellious. She'd been holding that stuff in all of that time, which was rough enough for her…not to mention, the fact that we held that secret even longer."

"Wow, Mitchell, I'm so sorry for all of you guys." Cheryl slowly shook her head from side to side. "Pastor, the thought of our baby girl being raped just tears my heart apart. It's really been rough, having to deal with her rebelliousness; and we just find out that she cuts herself-you know, **self-infliction**. It's like adding insult to injury. I just don't know how to deal with it."

"Cheryl, I'm going to tell you something, and I want you to listen to me-listen well. You all have got to show Lucy love. You all need to embrace her and talk to her. Let her know that you all love her regardless of what has happened to her. The last thing that she needs now is rejection." "I hear you, Pastor. We do love her, and we show her that. However, you just don't understand." "Yes, I do! I'm not saying to condone her rebelliousness towards you all. You all are her parents, and it's wrong for her to behave and disrespect you all that way.

Nevertheless, regardless of what type of sin one commits, we are to still love them just as God loves us. God's love is unconditional for us; and we must have that same attitude." Cheryl said, "I hear you, Pastor." "That's good, Cheryl; but I'm not done yet. As far as your comment about me not understanding you and Mitchell's situation, you couldn't imagine how much I do understand your situation.

Jan and I experienced the same thing a few years ago with our son. He became very rebellious. His soccer coach started molesting him when he was fourteen, but we didn't find out until right before his sixteenth birthday. You might remember when a coach was fired from Higher Heights' high school, for sexually abusing a student-but the student's family wanted to remain anonymous. Well, that was my family. Since my son was a minor, the media honored our request and didn't bother us." "Wow, Pastor, we had no idea that you all had gone through that." "Yep, and after that, that's when Lonnie became very rebellious; and he revealed to us that he was attracted to men.

During his senior year, we found out that he was dating a young man who'd graduated a year before him. He'd already gone off to college, and the two of them were planning to live together once Lonnie graduated high school. That's one of the reason we sent Lonnie to a school out of town-close to a thousand miles away. It was a trying time for all of us. However, with prayer, fasting, and showering Lonnie with love, we made it through it.

We as Christians, after we get saved, we learn to love people. However, sometimes with loving them, we become too trusting of people around us and some of them take advantage of that. We've got to be wise and watch and pray when it comes to our kids. I want to set up counseling sessions for the three of you." Cheryl and Mitchell thanked their Pastor.

CHAPTER FOUR
The Road To Freedom

When Lucy and her family had their first counseling session, Lucy opened up and vented all the things that she'd been holding inside to Pastor Dove. "The sexual abuse started when I was in 6th grade, and it continued until around my eight-grade year, when Mr. Bob moved away. I was so relieved to see him leave. I felt that he was no longer a threat.

However, I was ashamed to reveal to my parents the things he'd done to me. So, I just kept them inside until they confronted me about it, and I just couldn't keep it inside any longer." " Sweetie, you could've told us; we would've listened." "No, Cheryl, let her finish. This is her time, now," said Pastor Dove. "All of you will have an opportunity to express yourselves, but let Lucy pour out her heart first."

Cheryl lifted her hands. "Oh, I'm sorry." Pastor Dove pointed his hand toward Cheryl and said, "No, you're fine." He looked at Lucy and bowed his head. "Lucy, continue on." She said, "when I finally told my parents, I wanted them to keep it a secret and try to work it out among ourselves. We tried that for quite a while, but it didn't work. So, we realized at this point, that we all needed to get help to resolve the situation; and now, I'm glad that we did."

Once Lucy, Cheryl, and Mitchell were done expressing themselves, at the end of the session, Pastor Dove reminded them that one of the most important things that they had to do to be set free and healed, was to forgive Bob. By the time that they had their last session, the whole family had managed to forgive Bob for what he'd done to Lucy and had begun to heal.

When they had Bob's trial, although it was too late to convict him on charges for what he'd done to Lucy, she was used as a witness to testify of his character, to show what he was capable of doing. After the trial, Lucy felt closure in her life from all of the things that Mr. Bob had done to her. She felt at peace. No longer did fear grip her heart and guilt because she kept it a secret and surrendered to Mr. Bob without a fight. Although, she went with him out of fear, the thought of it still bothered her.

Even after all the counseling and her letting go of bitterness and unforgiveness that she once held against Mr. Bob, she still often, had thoughts about it. She felt like she needed closure, mentally. However, after the trial, she was set free mentally, and Mr. Bob physically became a prisoner in the State's Penitentiary.

The local news reported about Bob's trial on the day he went to court. Nigel was watching television, when a reporter went into details about the trial. He felt relieved to know that Bob was being sentenced for his crimes against kids. He felt relieved for Lucy and her parents. His heart had ached for them since the very first night that he'd met Mitchell at the restaurant, at the bar.

Although, it was too late for her name to be included in the indictment against him because the statute of limitations had expired, Bob's sentence made up for it. He was sentenced to spend so many years in prison until it was as if he'd been tried for Lucy's case, as well. A lot of people cheered after hearing the guilty verdict. Lucy and her parents were finally on the road to freedom.

CHAPTER FIVE
Bullying Has A Negative Effect

The family showed no emotions even though they had certainly suffered some major pain and challenges. However, Bob did apologize to Lucy and her family for the things he'd done to them all.

Nigel had a great heart for kids. He didn't like seeing them mistreated, or harmed in any way. He'd gone through a lot as a child, himself. From the time he started first grade until high school, he'd been bullied by some of his classmates. In first grade, he was made fun of for being so much taller than the other kids. He was also very slim, with a frail appearance.

After Nigel and his classmates had gotten a couple of years older, the teasing continued. During that time, the same kids would say that Nigel was so skinny because his family didn't have enough food at home-and that they were too poor to buy food for him to eat. Those particular kids knew nothing about Nigel's personal life. They were just being mean bullies. Nigel was actually a lot better off than they were, financially.

28

During Nigel's fifth grade year, his dad came to a parent-teacher's meeting for the first time because Nigel's mom always took care of that. The teacher just wanted to meet with his parents to discuss Nigel's progress in school, and to make sure he stayed on course with keeping up his grades. Nigel's mom was an average sized woman for her height. She was 5'5 and weighed 140 pounds. His dad, who his classmates saw for the first time, was 6'3 and weighed around 400 pounds, at that particular time. After his dad's visit to his school, some of his classmates (the usual bullies) started to tease him again, about why he was so skinny.

They had a new joke this time, an even crueler one. They said that they thought that his family was too poor to buy food for him, the reason that he was so skinny. However, they said that they had found out the real reason. They said that the real reason he was so skinny is because his dad was eating all of the food, leaving him nothing to eat.

What those very rude kids didn't know is that Nigel inherited his weight and height from his dad. Nigel's dad was

tall and skinny just like Nigel, up until
right after high school. While in high
school, he played football. Some people
felt that he would've made a great
basketball player because of his height.
However, he chose football.

He loved the game, and he dominated
it. By his senior year, he'd already earned
himself a bright future. The options he had
was that after graduation, he could either
accept a full paid scholarship to an Ivory
League college, or he had the option to
play NFL football, immediately after
graduating high school. However, injuries
sustained to both knees, during the last
game of his senior year, ruined his
opportunity to play football for any
colleges or the NFL. It took three months
of rehabilitation to get Nigel's dad back to
walking, again. By his graduation day, he
was able to walk with crutches. He walked
across the stage on crutches, and received
his high school diploma.

Although Nigel's dad wouldn't be
receiving a football scholarship, he still
wanted to go to college and further his
education. He eventually enrolled in
college a year later because he was busy

continuing his rehabilitation, for the
injuries to his knees. Nigel's mom was his
dad's high school sweet heart. She stuck
by him, and they got married shortly after
graduating college. Although, he received
physical therapy, his knees were never
quite the same. He became inactive, and
he gained a lot of weight throughout the
years, resulting in his weight of 400
pounds, at the time.

It was usually one or two kids in a
small group, who'd make rude remarks
about Nigel and his dad. Some of the
others in the group would just laugh,
which was just as bad. The bullying
continued throughout middle school. It
was really hard on Nigel to even have any
confidence because of all the bullying that
was going on. However, he was
determined to not let it affect him to the
point whereas he'd harm some of the kids
who'd been bullying him, or perhaps
himself, such as some of the kids he'd
heard about on the news.

After all the years of being bullied, by
the time Nigel started high school, he had
low self esteem. Unfortunately, some of
those same bullies from his previous

schools also attended high school with Nigel. They continued to bully Nigel all four years of high school. During the high school years, boys are usually interested in girls; and they like to impress them. For some guys, they like to impress them at the expense of hurting or humiliating other people. That's exactly what some of the same bullies did, who'd been ridiculing Nigel in the past.

However, this time the teasing continued because of Nigel's skin color. They'd especially, try to intimidate Nigel in front of girls. For instance, one of the bullies saw Nigel conversing with a girl. He and the usual group, walked over to them. Then, one of the boys yelled to the girl, "you need a real man. Ole high yellow, pretty boy, here, couldn't protect you if your life depended on it." One of the other guys said, "haaa! He'd be too busy trying to look pretty." A third boy joined in and said, "naw man, he'd fall over if someone just took a swing at him. They wouldn't even have to hit him, just the wind from the guy swinging at him would knock him down." The whole group laughed.

Nigel ignored them. He didn't think it was funny; neither did the girl. He and the girl walked away. She said to Nigel, "those guys are just jealous of you. Don't pay them any mind; and please don't allow them to provoke you to fight them. They'd probably use it as an opportunity to really hurt you, badly because they're just that jealous of you."

During Nigel's senior year, he was so fed up with all the bullying. He could hardly wait for his graduation ceremony. On graduation day, Nigel left his graduating class feeling proud of his accomplishments and carrying his high school diploma. However, he also left carrying years of hurt and pain, from all of the ridicule he'd endured from some of his classmates, all of his school years.

Nigel carried all that pain over into adulthood. It really affected his life, but it wasn't obvious to others. They were busy admiring him and wishing for a similar good life.

After high school, Nigel decided to do something that was really challenging for him. He wanted to get his past off his mind and move forward. So, he chose to enroll in the Marine Corps; that happened after his first year in college. He still continued his college education and received a Master's Degree.

After Nigel was discharged from the Marine Corps and had gotten a corporate job, he realized his issues from the past were still very much affecting him. He'd worked with his colleagues, daily, and he managed to smile and hide his pain. The people who knew his personally, didn't notice his issues, either. Some of his close family members did notice his behavior during certain situations, but even they didn't know the extent of his issues.

There were times when Nigel would see some of his classmates (the ones that weren't kind to him), and he wouldn't go out of his way to speak to them. One particular classmate walked up to Nigel and spoke to him. Nigel spoke, but he purposely, acted as though he didn't remember the individual. He felt a little guilty afterwards. He knew he was wrong for that. He ended up laughing about it, though.

As time moved on, Nigel could feel
bitterness just building in his heart toward
the individuals that had ridiculed and
bullied him, for so many years. He'd
gotten to the point whereas he didn't want
to see nor even be around any of his
classmates. Seeing them brought back the
bad memories of the past. He would have
flashbacks about some of the times when
he was extremely humiliated; and he'd get
emotional. Whenever he'd think about that
part of his life from the past, he'd feel bad.
He would actually feel anger and
bitterness toward those involved in any
way, including those that laughed and
seemed amused at seeing people ridicule
him, as well as those who actually did it.

One day when Nigel had a flashback of
his past, he noticed like never before the
rage that he felt. Then, it hit him like a ton
of bricks that he had unforgiveness in his
heart, and he needed to let it go. He knew
that it wasn't right and it wasn't healthy
for him to keep allowing unforgiveness to
remain in his heart. In the past, he would
even get teased after he'd attended church
services. Some of the kids that attended
the same church as he did would tease him
in school, the next day. His pain certainly

ran deep; he'd probably never forget it.
However, he needed to let go of
unforgiveness.

When Nigel realized that he needed to
forgive his classmates and others that had
hurt him, he also realized that he didn't
know how. He really did not know how to
forgive. Even though he wanted to do it
for all the right reasons, he still felt the
urge inside to remain bitter and hold on to
unforgiveness, no matter how hard he
desired to let it go.

Nigel realized that the time had come
for him to vent…to reveal to someone his
secret, about how all of the pain and hurt
he'd experienced had affected his life. He
needed to share how he'd become bitter
and was holding unforgiveness against the
people who'd hurt him. He was planning
to confess how that once he realized that,
and wanted to forgive those people, he
honestly, didn't know how to forgive.

After thinking about someone to talk to
about his situation, Nigel decided to talk to
his God about it. Nigel opened up to the
Lord about his situation. He repented, and
he remembered what the bible says about

having to forgive others, or God wouldn't forgive our sins. He told the Lord that he wanted to forgive, but he didn't know how. He asked God to help him and to show him how to forgive. The Lord heard Nigel's cry, and he helped him. **He told Nigel to open his mouth and confess,** ***"Lord, I forgive everyone for all I have against them in my heart, and Lord, forgive me for all of my sins."***

Immediately, after Nigel said those words, he felt a release on the inside, in his spirit. Nigel never imagined that letting go was that simple-just by simply opening his mouth and declaring it, even though he wasn't feeling it at first. However, afterwards, he felt it immediately.

He still had memories sometimes, of the humiliating events of his past and he realized that some people are still the same, in some ways. He knew that just because you forgave people, it didn't necessarily mean that they'd changed. Therefore, he knew that it was his choice to use wisdom, when making the decision whether or not to be around them. Nevertheless, the main thing is that he no longer held bitterness and unforgiveness in his heart against anyone.

Nigel finally decided to share his experiences with his mom. He called her before hoping on his motorcycle and heading over to his dad's and her home. Brrrrrr-brrrrrr, brrrrr-brrrrr. "Now, who is this? Nobody calls until I'm busy. Oh, it's Nigel. Hey!" "Hi mom; what are you doing?" "I was just folding some clothes; what's going on?" "Everything is lovely…just wanted to come over and talk to you about something, if it's not a bad time." "Of course not! I always have time for my only son-well, my only child. Ha, ha! Boy, bring yourself over here! Your dad's not here, right now, but we can still talk. I'll see you, shortly." "Okay, mom, I'm on my way…talk to you, later." "Okay, Nigel…bye."

Nigel walked into his garage, picked up his helmet and put it on. He opened his garage door, started his Honda RC213V-S and slowly pulled it out. Then, he shut his garage door back and rode off to his parents' house. The ride there was a pleasant one. It was a beautiful day, and the breeze felt cool and refreshing to his skin as he rode his motorcycle.

Nigel made it to his parents' house quickly, on his motorcycle. He drove into their drive way, parked his bike, shut it off and went inside their house. His mom was standing in the doorway as he went inside. They gave each other a big hug. "Nigel, you can come on into the family room. I'm just watching a little t.v., while I fold clothes. Your dad is still out and about. He went to get his hair cut, and there's no telling how many other places he's stopped off at. So, I don't know what time he'll get back home." "Oh...no problem, mom; I'm good. I mean, I-I kind of wanted to just talk to you, anyway." "Oh, okay; well, let me cut this television off so I can give you my undivided attention."

She reached over beside her, on the couch, got the remote and cut off the television. "Wait just one minute." She leaned forward and reached for a glass of water that was sitting on a coffee table, on a coaster, right in front of her. She took a sip of cool water, and slid back in the couch. "Okay, now, I'm ready. My ears are opened!"

Nigel was trying to figure out where to start. He paused for a couple of seconds, and then, he finally began to tell her his story. He told her how badly he was mistreated by his classmates and how he'd carried the pain for years. He told her how he'd allowed bitterness and unforgiveness to develop in his heart against them.

He chose to open up and converse with his mom about it because even though there are some things that only a male can relate to concerning another man, there seems to be a special bond between a male child and his mom. It's usually the same way with a daughter and dad. That's one of the reasons that Nigel felt comfortable talking to his mom the way that he did.

After hearing some of the things that Nigel had said to her, his mom replied, "wow, son! I know you'd mentioned to me once, when you were a little boy, how that some of the kids had said some rude things about you. You may remember me telling you to ignore them and just say, 'sticks and stones may break my bones, but words

will never hurt me.'" "Yeah, mom, I
remember that." "Well, that's what our
folks always told us to say when we were
teased or made fun of. They meant well.
They were trying to help us cope with
situations like that, and especially during a
time when we were growing up in the
south, during the Jim-Crow era.

Black folks suffered a lot back then;
and it wasn't all from white folks, but it
was from some people of our own race.
Just like today, some of them were jealous
of each other and were afraid that some
others might obtain more than what they
had. They had what's known as the 'crab
in the bucket' syndrome. Therefore, some
of them would do whatever they could to
try and pull some other people down, even
if it came to speaking rude and evil about
them."

Nigel's mom paused momentarily, as
though she was in deep thought. "Yep, so
to cope with any verbal attacks against us,
our folks told us to say that words would
never hurt us. For years, now, that has
been passed down to different generations,
but it's one of the biggest-I would say,
'lies,' but instead, I'll say, 'deceptions,'

told to anyone. I said that to make this point, words definitely do hurt. They can do damage to people's lives." His mom reached out and gave her son a big hug.

"Well, son, I'm glad that you got help. I'm glad you got deliverance from the things that were hurting you, and that you are finally able to let go of the bitterness and unforgiveness, that were in your heart. I've been there-done that; and God is good. It just goes to show though, that you can't judge a book by its cover. I had no ideal you were hurting like you were. You always seemed upbeat, was always smiling, with your handsome self. You get your good looks from your mom. Ha, ha, ha!

It makes you wonder though, when you see all the smiling faces and well groomed, attractive people, walking pass you daily-just how many are really hurting on the inside. It makes you wonder how many are carrying secrets and experiencing pain from something like what you've gone through. I mean, when you see people with the look of distress on their faces and behaving a certain way, that makes it kind of obvious that something not so good, is going on in their lives. However, some folks may be fooling us by their nice outward appearance."

When Nigel's mom mentioned about the look of distress, he immediately thought about the look of distress on Mitchell's face, the first time he'd met him at the bar. His mom continued on making her point. "However, those type people whose appearances allows them to hide pain and other things, you'd never know what's going on with them unless they tell someone, or the Lord reveals it. I'm just saying." She shook her head.

Nigel held in his bottom lip for a second, before saying, "well, mom, I'd better get going. I have a long day ahead of me, tomorrow. I've got to do some final tweaking of a proposal that I plan to present on tomorrow." He reached out and hugged his mom. "I love you, mom. Give dad my love as well, when he gets in. I'll talk to you later." "Okay, son, I'll see you later."

When Nigel went to work the next day, he displayed his usual smile and upbeat personality. However, this time he was being genuine with his colleagues. They were getting a genuinely, happy smile, and not one to help mask pain. They were beholding a person with an upbeat personality because he was free inside. He was truly alive. He knew that criticism would come; but he knew then, how to forgive those that offended him. He'd learned and experienced more about the true love of God.

The older saints used to say that the devil knew what God was doing or about to do in your life, and that's why he tries to get you off course. They'd say that, sometimes, the devil would use other people who were walking in carnality to get to you. Well, that proved to be the case with Nigel after he got to work, feeling good.

He met with his colleagues in the company's conference room; he passed out an outline of his proposal to each person in the meeting. After that, he made his presentation and put his proposal before everyone. Then, he gave them each an opportunity to give their input on the presentation.

However, one of his colleagues, Brian, aggressively began to challenge the things that Nigel had said. It was like he was irate with Nigel. You could just see the devil using him. He said to Nigel, in a very snappy way, "what are you trying to do?! I mean-I don't get it." Nigel said, "what is it that you don't get? I purposely went out of my way to carefully clarify everything that I presented to you all. So, is there anyone else who also didn't comprehend the things that I presented before you? Please raise your hands if so-because if there are enough of you that didn't understand, I'll go back over my proposal."

None of his other colleagues raised their hands. Brian, quickly responded, "I comprehended it, but I just don't understand what you're looking to accomplish." Nigel said, "I gave each of you an outline of my proposal before I made my presentation. Since you seem to be the only one who didn't get what I was saying, then, I suggest that you read it alone, yourself. Perhaps you'll be able to grasp it better that way."

It was obvious that there was more to the situation than what Brian was ranting about. However, Nigel wasn't about to entertain that foolishness; and he kindly shut him down. "Brian, sometimes, I have to do that myself. Sometimes, in order for me to fully get what's being said, I have to read back over it several times. Sometimes, that's just what you have to do to get some things to make any sense to you. Believe me, you're not along."

Some of Nigel's other colleagues looked around at each other. One could clearly see the disgusted look on Brian's face. His behavior caught Nigel off guard.

However, after a few minutes of Brian's ranting and drama, Nigel knew who was behind Brian's behavior…no one but the devil. As the old saints would say, "aint nobody mad but the devil."

Nigel had never had any issues with Brian before that day, and he overlooked his rudeness and forgave him for his nasty behavior towards him. After Brian's behavior, and since everyone else understood, there was really no reason to

CHAPTER SIX
Favor

prolong the meeting. So, Nigel declared that the meeting was over. He dismissed everyone so that they could go back to their offices, look back over his proposal, and give him their decisions by the next business day.

When Nigel arrived at work the next day, he greeted his colleagues with a smile. He spoke to them all, as usual. He found out that his proposal had been approved by everyone, including Brian. That decision was going to bring in lots of capital for the company and a hefty bonus for Nigel. Nigel just shook his head and thanked God in his heart for **favor,** and for helping him to not behave unseemly when Brian so rudely challenged him, the day before.

Nigel had a great day at work. The workday ended really fast. Time just seems to fly when you're having fun. As Nigel was leaving from work, he called his mom. Brrrrr-brrrrrr. His mom picked up on the second ring. "Hello!" "Hi, mom; I'm just letting you know that I'll be heading over there, shortly. I want to talk to you about something; it's nothing bad. It's actually good news." "Okay." "I'll be there as soon as I stop off and have me a good ole pina colada, ha, ha, ha! ...okay?" "Yeah, that's okay. I'll be here. Your dad is here, too." "Oh, okay, cool! I'll talk to you shortly, then." "Okay, Nigel."

Nigel went to his usual spot and had a pina colada; then, he headed to his parents' place. When Nigel arrived at his parent's home and rang their doorbell, his dad answered the door. "Hey, stranger; oops, I mean dad. Ha, ha, ha! What you been up to old man?" "Watch it, now! Who are you calling an old man?" He reached out and grabbed Nigel's neck and put him in a headlock. Both of them were standing there looking like two tall trees. Nigel couldn't do anything but surrender. "Wow! Dad, you still got it, man."

They both chuckled as they walked into the family room, where Nigel's mom was sitting. "Hey mom!" Nigel walked over and gave her a big hug. "Hey, have a seat, son." Nigel took a seat on the couch. "I just wanted to share with you how the Lord has been blessing me. You know how God set me free from bitterness and unforgiveness, that I'd been holding against some folks because of the hurtful things they'd done to me.

Anyhow, the very next day, the devil just acted up in one of my colleagues. I mean, I've never had any problems with this guy before; his name is Brian. When I went in to work and gave my presentation for my proposal, he just out of the blue, became so aggressive in his speech towards me. He was just determined to challenge and debate the things I'd presented before the group. I'd never seen him behave like that before, especially towards me.

It startled me for a minute; but after a moment or so of hearing him ranting and acting as if he was angry with me, I realized it was the devil using him. I didn't argue with him; I used wisdom in the way that I responded to him and at the end of the day, I forgave him. I dismissed everybody so that they could go back to their offices and review the outline for my proposal that I'd given to them. I did that so that they could give me an answer by the next business day, which was today, of course.

Nevertheless, I left work holding no grudges against Brian. I went home, had dinner, soaked in the tub for a while, and I got in bed. I didn't even worry about it. Well, when I went in to work on today, I got the good news that everyone including Brian, had voted yes to my proposal. After the way he behaved, I really didn't know what to expect from him, but God...! Ha, ha, ha! God is so good." His mom replied, "oh yes, he is!"

"Also, let me tell you all this, being that they approved my proposal, that's going to bring in big bucks for the company. In addition to that, I'll get a hefty bonus." "Oh yeah, that was the devil that caused that man to rise up against you like that. He doesn't want to see you blessed; but when the **favor** of God is on your life, you don't have to worry about what people say. When God bless you, no man can curse you." His dad nodded his head and replied, "oh yeah, aint nobody mad but the devil, about how God is blessing you. You just keep doing what's right and right will follow you-in other words, you'll reap what you sow, son."

"I hear the both of you; I hear you loud and clear, and I plan to do just that, dad. Well, ok, I just wanted to share my testimony with you guys. I'm about to head home, shower and hit the sack. I love you guys." Nigel hugged his parents. They walked with him to the door. He got in his vehicle and drove home, showered and hit the sack, just as he said he'd do.

After Nigel left, his parents sat around discussing how proud they were of his accomplishments. Nigel's dad said to Nigel's mom, "Mrs. Austella, I'm proud of that son that you birthed into this world. He's my only child; and he's making me real proud." "I hear you, daddy." Mrs. Austella smiled. "I'm also very proud of him. He looks up to you, a lot, too. I can tell that he's glad that you got serious about your health, and lost all that weight while he was away in the Marine Corps. He was worried about your health.

You're strong as a bull now, though. Ha, ha, ha!" "Oh yeah, mama, he got a taste of it tonight, too; I put that rascal in a headlock. He couldn't do anything but surrender and laugh." "Haaa...with his tall self-looking just like you. I tease with him sometimes, about him getting his good looks from me, but he's just like you. Chile, it looks just like you spit him out!" "Yeah, that's what everybody say, whenever we're together. When they say it, I just smile from ear to ear because I'm one proud father." "Yep, and he's proud for you to be his father."

Mrs. Austella leaned over and kissed her husband's right cheek, grabbed him by the hands, and pulled him up. "Come on, let's go shower and get some rest." He followed behind her and replied, "it's a good thing we have double showers because I'd be up all night waiting on my turn to get in." "Ha, haaa! I'm not even going there with you, tonight." "Well, you know it's true." They both chuckled and got in the shower.

They both took a nice, warm shower, dried off, put on deodorant and lotion. Mrs. Austella dabbed on a little La vie est belle. It smelled sooo good. Mrs. Austella said, "baby, some people mind just get all over the page when I happen to mention that we have double showers." Mr. Austella replied, "yep, baby, my mind is all over the page right about now, too.

Ha, ha, ha!" "You are so silly. Good night, baby." "Good night my wonderful, darling wife."

"Hey baby, I was just thinking, whatever became of the girl that Nigel was dating when he first got back here from serving time, in the Marine Corps?" "Good night, dear. I don't know; ask him the next time you talk to him. Good ni-iiight." "Okay, good night," said Mrs. Austella.

A few minutes later, Mrs. Austella said, "baby, you know I was just thinking that Nigel needs a wife. Our baby needs to get married." "He's not a baby. He's a grown man." "Yep, and a grown man needs a good wife. I was just thinking about Vickie's daughter; you know Vickie that goes to church with us. It's her daughter, she'll be a good match for Nigel.

She's a sweet little girl, and she speaks to me whenever she sees me. She's even asked about Nigel a few times. They're both good kids. They have that in common." "Why are you trying to play match-maker? Also, Vickie's daughter is not a little girl. She's a grown woman just like Nigel is a grown man. Why do you keep trying to make these grown folks be kids?" "Baby, you know what I mean. Compared to our age, they're young. So, I just call them kids." "You're right; they are young...young adults! That's what you need to refer to them as-young adults. I'm sure neither one of them would want to be referred to as kids, especially Nigel.

Men are sensitive to that kind of stuff, especially the real 'grown men', like the one we've raised." "Okay, I see what you're saying. I get the point; and I'll stop doing that." "It's okay. It's nothing major. We have to check each other, at times. You're my wife, and I love you; and I just don't want someone else to tell you in a rude way and hurt your feelings." "I totally understand what you're saying; and I will do better...sorry for talking so much. I just had those things on my mind and wanted to get them off my chest."

"No problem; I understand, honey. Now, come on and let me take care of you so we won't be up all night." "What do you mean?" "You know what I mean! Ha, ha, ha!" "Oh, I'm good. I'm about to go to sleep, now." "Okay, if you say so," said Mr. Austella as he smiled and shook his head. "Good night, woman." Mrs. Austella smiled as well and said, "Good night, baby." They both rolled over in bed, and got a good night's sleep.

The next morning when Mr. and Mrs. Austella woke up, they turned on the news to catch the weather report and to see what was going on in their city. Chicago was no stranger to crime, but they wanted to see what exactly was going on.

As they watched the news, a female reporter began reporting on a hostage situation at a restaurant. She reported that someone attempted to rob a crowded restaurant and its customers. There was a large group fellowshipping at dinner, together, on that day because they were having their class reunion the next day. All of the customers' cell phones were taken so that they couldn't call for help.

It became a hostage situation after one man from the group of classmates got away from the robbers. He was pistol whipped badly, in the head, but he managed to fight off the robbers enough to break free from their hold. He was alive

CHAPTER SEVEN
The Robbery

and expected to make it, but he was at a trauma center a few miles from the restaurant.

As the Austell's watched more of that story, they saw that the group of classmates was Nigel's graduating class. Also, the guy that was pistol whipped and hospitalized in serious condition, they recognized him. Nigel wasn't in attendance because he didn't keep in touch with his classmates. After the bad way that some of them treated him, he hardly kept in touch with any of them. Mrs. Austella sent him a text though, to let him know what happened.

The next day when Nigel went to work, he heard bits and pieces about the hostage situation, from some of his colleagues. However, it wasn't enough information for him to know that it was a large number of folks from his graduating class, who were at the restaurant during **the robbery**. Nobody at his job had time to really get into the story while at work because they were all busy. Also, Nigel didn't check his text messages until late that evening, after work. So, he didn't know that it was his graduating class that were in the middle of the hostage situation until late that evening, after reading his mom's text. His mom had mentioned in the text that he'd recognize the guy that got pistol whipped, and was in the hospital, in serious condition. After reading that part of the text, Nigel started to get somewhat concerned that perhaps that guy may have been one of the few people that did treat him nicely, while attending school together.

Nigel was late reading his text. So, he immediately responded to his mother's message to let her know that he'd contact someone from his graduating class to get more information about the situation. Nigel made sure he watched the news that night, and he did find out more information about the incident.

The news reported that there were two robbery suspects involved, and that they eventually surrendered. Those held hostage, were escorted by law officials and paramedics were waiting for them, outside. Paramedics checked all of the people who gave them permission to do so. They checked things such as their blood pressure and heart rates. Each person that they checked, were asked if they had diabetes; and they checked for any signs of issues with those particular individuals that had it.

The news also reported the name of the guy who was whipped in the head with a pistol. They said that he remained in the hospital, in serious-but stable condition. They also reported that his injuries were non-life threatening.

Nigel was relieved to hear that news, and he still planned to contact someone from his class, especially the guy in the hospital. Nigel did recognize him, and he wasn't one of the people who were cool with Nigel, during the time that they'd attended high school together. However, Nigel saw this as a chance to show the love of God and forgiveness to him.

The guy's name was Gregory. Nigel and other people called him Greg, for short. He'd given Nigel a hard time in the past. He would tease and bully Nigel about his light skinned complexion, called him a pretty boy, and even made several

attempts to provoke him to fight him.
Nigel wasn't afraid of him and he stood up
for himself, but he chose not to participate
in such foolishness, which didn't amount
to anything but trouble. His parents raised
him well, with class and respect for others.
Nigel was a swell guy.

Nigel called the hospital to see if
Gregory was allowed to receive visitors.
The receptionist told Nigel that he could
visit with Gregory. Nigel asked that she
connect him to his room, and she did.

When Greg answered the phone, Nigel
let him know who he was, and Greg was
glad to hear from him. They conversed for
a while, and Nigel let him know before
they ended their conversation, that he'd
visit with him the next day. Greg replied,
"yeah man, come by; I'll be glad to see
you." Greg hadn't seen Nigel since he
returned to Chicago from the Marine
Corps. Nigel said, "okay man, I'll talk to
you tomorrow, then." They both hung up
their phones. Greg was sincerely happy to
hear from Nigel. Nigel felt pretty good
himself. He didn't feel any bitterness
towards Greg.

He went to the hospital to visit Greg
the next day. Greg was elated to see him.
When Nigel walked in, he went over to
Greg's bed; they shook hands and very
briefly, hugged each other. Nigel took a
seat in a chair that was in the room. Greg
had the television on in his room.

The news kept continuously reporting
on the hostage situation that had occurred.
Nigel said to Greg, "I'm sure glad you're
going to be okay. It could've been worse."
"Yeah, I know, man. I'm glad to still be
here. My adrenaline was pumping, and I
made a run for it. They tried to stop me,
but when I wouldn't stop, one of the guys
started beating me on the head with his
pistol. That thing sure did hurt, too, but I
kept fighting until I got out of there so I
could get some help. They had taken all of
our cell phones. They even pulled the
restaurant phone out the wall.

I used to get a lot of spankings from my
dad for being so aggressive and fighting
all the time, when I was younger, but that
was one time being a fighter helped save
my life. When I think back over the
situation, those dudes were crazy and
didn't care about nothing. They could've

killed me." Nigel paused for a second and replied, "yeah, there was that possibility, but God…to God be the Glory, that you made it out of there alive. God is good." "Yes he is! I'm gonna turn off this t.v., for a while. I'm tired of watching them showing the robbery over and over again." He shook his head.

"Hey Nigel, man look, I want to say this to you…been wanting to say it for a long time, now. I know I did a lot of stuff that wasn't cool to you, when we were in high school. I used to try my best to get you mad enough to fight me because I wanted to just beat you down, man."

When Greg said that, Nigel thought to himself about how he did beat him down, verbally, and it sure did hurt; but he survived it. Greg continued on, "man, I was jealous of you. You were tall and good looking. You were light skinned; and those girls were crazy about y'all light skinned dudes. A really dark skinned guy like me didn't stand a chance back then. Y'all light skinned dudes were in-back then." Nigel said, "well I hate to burst your bubble, but we're baack, and we're here to stay, this time. Ha, ha, ha!"

Greg said, "yeah, you're right, man. They love us chocolate brothers too, now; but it was certainly different back then. We dark skinned brothers just didn't have a chance, man…kind of like how it was with the thick girls. A few dudes would talk to them, but for the most part, they went after the average sized girls and the skinny chicks.

We were young then, but when I think back, maaan, some of those thick girls looked good, and they look even better now that I've learned some sense. I saw one of those sisters the other day; she had on a dress, and those thick, beautiful legs were banging. I could hardly drive for looking. I look at it like this, we're all equal. Everybody has their own preference, you know…to each his own."

Nigel said, "yeah, you're right about that." Greg resumed speaking, "as I was saying though, Nigel, I was sooo jealous of your looks, but for the most part, I think your character got to me the most. Man, you were so classy; you never had a bad word to say, about anyone. Man, your parents raised you right. Out of all the teasing and putting folks down that the other guys did, you had no part in that. It was like you had the confidence within yourself, that you didn't need to put anyone else down, to try and make yourself look good."

"Greg, bruh, you just don't know. I had no confidence in that sense. The little confidence I did have, you all destroyed that with all the constant teasing. I tried to hold on to it, but by high school, my self-esteem was at an all-time low. It wasn't that I was so confident in the sense you're talking about. It was just that my parents taught me to treat people right-the way I wanted to be treated, and I did that.

So, at the end of the day, I could hold my head up high with confidence, knowing that I'd treated people right. That's what you witnessed. That's the type of confidence that you saw-not confidence about the way I looked. I still strive today, to treat people right and show people respect." "You put some respect on it, huh?" Nigel replied, "for sho!" "Yeah, and I respect you for that. Man, please forgive me for all the evil stuff I said about you and the way I treated you the whole time. I'm sorry." "You know what Greg? I've already forgiven you. Your apology is accepted. I love you, man. God bless you." "God bless you too, Nigel." They shook hands, again.

Nigel laughed and said, "my chocolate brother or as the ladies would say, 'chocolate eye candy.'" They both burst out in laughter. Greg said, "yeah man, that's what they call us, now. Sometimes, when I go in stores, or just out and about, I hear women talking about me.

One day, it was two of them watching me. I knew they were watching me. So, I was listening hard, man. Ha, ha, ha…so I could hear what they were saying, if they were talking about me. One of the ladies told the other one while looking me up and down, 'girl, chocolate is my weakness. Umm-ump! Do you see that piece of candy over there?!'" "Then, the other lady looked over at me and said, 'how can you miss him?! Girl, I'd better get out of here before I get in trouble.'" "The one that started it all said, 'chile, I better leave my own self. Ha, ha, ha!'" "Then, they both walked away."

Nigel said, "yeah, man, I'm telling you, these women now days are so bold. I'm old fashioned. If a woman is interested in me, I don't mind at all if she makes it known, but I'd prefer that she did it, subtly. I had one young lady that came on to me so strong until it actually kind of scared me. All I ask is that they keep it lady like. Honestly, I prefer to make the first move, but a lot has changed. So, I try to be open- about some things...not about all this crazy stuff some people want you to be down with, now days."

Greg shook his head. "I know what you mean! I was secretly dating a woman when I lived in Wisconsin. I didn't set out to date her. We were just friends at first; she was married. However, we both were attracted to each other, but we tried to pretend as if we weren't. We kept saying that we were just friends, but we both knew what was up. One day, she told me that she wanted us to only be friends, for real! You get what I'm saying?" Nigel nodded his head and said, "Yeah, I gotcha." "She said that she'd rather see someone who was married like her because they'd have more in common. She said that she felt they both would be more

understanding of each other's-other
obligations.

Now, by that time, I had started having
some strong feelings for her. I mean, don't
get me wrong; I knew it wasn't going
anywhere, and I'm not about trying to
break up anybody's home. So, as long as I
could see her and spend some time with
her, I was good. I knew what was up and
that it could end any minute, but I wasn't
ready for that, man. It hurt me, but I'm a
grown man, and I wasn't about to be
crying and letting her know my feelings
like that.

Anyhow, I eventually decided to move
back here to Chicago, but it had nothing to
do with our situation. I still talked to her at
times, but it was different. I still had
feelings for her that were hard to let go of.
However, besides the fact that she was
married, she'd distanced herself from me.
So, when I got ready to move back here, I
felt a sense of relief, like that was my way
out of it all. I felt like that was my way out
of having to be around her and at the same
time, still struggling with the feelings that
I had for her. Therefore, I told her that I
would be leaving, soon. The day I left, I

said to her, 'I'll be leaving today, and you take care.'"

"To my surprise, she said, 'okay, but you have my number; you've got all my contact information. I want you to keep in touch with me.'" "I was surprised-you know, things had changed between us because that's what she said that she wanted. However, when she saw I was leaving, she wanted us to keep in touch. Bruh, I had to look out for me. I threw up them duces on my way out, and I haven't looked back since." "Wow! I know you may have felt some type of way, at first, but you did the best thing."

"Yeah, I know I did…and I feel better, too. I gotta admit though, ole girl had me feeling ways that she would never even imagine. Nevertheless, I'm glad that I was able to fight and do what was right and what was best for me."

Nigel said, "Well Greg, man, I've got to run…got some things to take care of. It seems I can never get anything done during the week, unless I take off work. I'm always busy. I have to use the weekends to get anything done.

If it's something like business-something
that I have no choice but to take care of
during the week, then, I'll take off work.
Otherwise, I'm grinding, man." "Hey, I
clearly understand. I'm the same way-
hustle and flow.

The company that I work for laid off a
lot of folks, earlier this year. I'm just
thankful to God that I'm still hanging in
there. Sometimes, the work can get a little
tedious, but for the most part, it's good.
I'm not complaining. I'm just glad to still
have a job. The Lord blessed me not to get
laid off. God is good, man." " Yes, he is.
I'll see you later, Greg." "Okay, man, I'm
glad you stopped by. I'm gonna tell the
guys that I saw you."

As Nigel was walking the down the
hall, on his way out of the hospital, He
saw two more of his classmates. They
were actually a couple. They'd gotten
married right after college, but Nigel had
no idea that they'd gotten married.
Immediately, when they all saw each
other, they recognized one another.
Maureen yelled, "hey stranger! Ha, ha, ha!
Nigel Austella, it's been ages since I've
seen you, boi." Nigel smiled. "Yes, it has

been a while." Maureen used to have a
big time crush on Nigel, back in the day.

Maureen's husband, Dennis, walked
over to Nigel and shook his hand. "Nigel,
it's good to see you again, man. It's been a
long time. I don't think I've seen you
since graduation day. I know somebody
told me you'd enlisted in the army."
"Yeah, well…the Marine Corps." "Oh,
okay. So, how did that work for you?"

"Well, I served two terms in the
Marines-one of which I did a tour of duty
in Iraq. I actually liked it until after my
second term, when I served time in Iraq.
Although I liked it, had I served my tour
of duty in Iraq during my first term, I
don't think I would've signed up for a
second term. It was good for that time, but
I knew eventually, it was time for me to
move on. I continued my college
education while I was in there, and got a
master's. So, immediately when I got out,
I successfully obtained a corporate
position with a major company, right here
in downtown Chicago." "Oh wow! Man,
that's great. I'm glad for you." "Yeah, I
thank God for it, Dennis."

Dennis never knew about Maureen's crush on Nigel, but her body language was definitely telling the story.

Maureen listened, quietly, as they continued to talk before interrupting the two of them. "Nigel, I hate to run, but we gotta go visit someone." "Oh, okay. You all must be going to see Greg, right? I just left him, a few minutes ago." Maureen said, "oh, you did?!" "Yeah, and he was in good spirits. He's going to be okay. He'll be just fine." Dennis said, "oh, okay, that's good to hear. I guess you heard about the robbery and hostage situation, then, huh? It's been all over the news." "Yeah, well, my mom told me about it. She and my dad had seen it on the news a couple of days ago. I actually had not seen it on the news until then. My mom knew that I knew Greg, and she texted me.

Some of my colleagues were talking about it on the job; but they only had bits and pieces about it-not enough to put the whole story together. When I went home that evening and checked my text messages, I had a text from my mom. She'd given me the information I needed to learn more about the situation, and to get to visit with Greg." "Okay, well you take care, Nigel." Nigel replied, "alright, likewise to you, Dennis, and you too, Maureen." Maureen took a good look at Nigel as she replied, "Okay, bye, Nigel."

Nigel headed home, and Dennis and Maureen headed to Greg's room. Dennis walked into Greg's room with Maureen right behind him. "What it is dawg?!" "You got it, man. Ha, ha, ha!" Maureen said, "Hi, Greg." "Hey, girl! How've you've been?" "I'm good; I can't complain." "Well, that's good to hear. I can't complain my own self. I'm just glad things are as well as they are.

Girl, you'd better have a seat…you too, Dennis. Man, y'all get a couple of those chairs and pull around so we can talk. Nigel just left. I was sure glad to see him. Bruh looking good, too man." "Yeah, we saw him in the hall and talked to him for a little while, and he told us that he'd just left from visiting with you. He told me that he'd been in the Marines and served a tour in Iraq. Man, I didn't know that. I knew I'd heard somebody mention that he'd gone in the army or something, but I had no idea he'd gone in the Marine

Corps. Man, much respect…nothing but much respect for him." "Yep, the same here, man…nothing but respect for the brother." Maureen said, "Yeah I was glad to see Nigel…hadn't seen him in a long time." Greg said, "yeah, that's right, Maureen, you used to, um…." Greg paused because he thought about perhaps Dennis didn't know about Maureen's strong crush that she had on Nigel, back in the day.

It was the past and all, but you just never know how some folks will react to that kind of stuff. Greg almost put his foot in his mouth, but he stopped just in time to play it off. "Maureen, you used to be in the same class with Nigel, too, weren't you?" Maureen realized what was going on, and she played it off, too. "Yeah, I was…." "Yeah, I thought I remember you being in the same class…."

It wouldn't have really made a difference had they revealed that Maureen once had a crush on Nigel. Dennis was a little jealous…typical stuff, but nothing major. If anything, he'd probably have gotten more upset if he'd known they were trying to hide it from him.

The three of them continued conversing throughout the night until visiting hours were over. A lady's voice could be heard over the intercom, saying, "visiting hours are now, over. Please make your way out of the patients' rooms. Thanks for your cooperation."

Dennis said, "alright now, I'm glad you're going to be okay. We're about to get up out of here. You should be going home, soon, shouldn't you?" "Yeah, I was talking to a nurse earlier this morning, and she said that I might be leaving tomorrow, if everything is still looking okay." "Oh, okay, well, that's good, man. We'll see you, then." "Alright, Dennis…glad y'all stopped by. Bye, Maureen." "Bye, Greg. You take care, now." "Alright, I'm about to hit the sack if they let me. Seems like every time I try to fall asleep, one of the nurses come in to check my vitals or something. Ha, ha, ha! Good night, y'all."

Dennis and Maureen told Greg good night and walked down the hall heading to their car. They were glad they got to see him and that he was going to be okay. Things could've turned out worse.

CHAPTER EIGHT
Nigel's Choice

As they exited the hospital, Maureen said, "baby, I didn't want to say anything to Nigel or Greg, but I was shocked to see that those two were getting along. I'm not saying this because of anything Nigel did; it was Greg that was a hot mess.

I don't know if you remember how Greg used to give Nigel a hard time, when we were in high school. He acted like he couldn't stand Nigel…like he hated his guts; but I see Nigel still has class. He was right here at this hospital to check on Greg just like we were, as if nothing ever happened.

Greg was so evil; he treated Nigel like a dog. Some people would've still been bitter. They wouldn't have come this way, to visit him; but I see that Nigel chose to forgive him. I know God had to help him. I imagine he did plenty of praying to get to this point, so that he could do what was right. Whatever the case was, **Nigel's choice** was the right one, to forgive."

"So, was it serious?" Maureen replied with a puzzled look on her face, "was what serious?" Dennis said, "whatever you and Nigel had going on, in the past." "You know I loved myself some Nigel-me and a lot of other girls! We dated a few times, but it was not serious." "I never knew any of that; I just noticed your body language, earlier." "…my body language?! Man, please-whatever!"

"For real though…." "Okay, if you say so, Dennis." Maureen frowned and shook her head. By that time, they had made it to their car. Dennis walked to the passenger side, opened the door for Maureen, and she got inside. Dennis closed the door for her, walked around to the driver's side, and opened his door. He got in his car, closed his door, and cranked the car.

Maureen looked over at Dennis and said, "I just want you to know that as nice as Nigel is, you have nothing to worry about. I have the person that I know God intended for me to have. Also, I have the person that I love and desire to spend the rest of my life with. I wouldn't want it to be any other way." "Right! I didn't just fall off the turnip truck." Dennis chuckled. "Naw, for real though, I wasn't worried. I just noticed your reaction, and I was

curious. That's all it was. I trust you, girl."
"I appreciate that. That's good to hear.
Besides, there are enough single women
out there for Nigel to choose from that
would be glad to have him as a husband,
just as I'm glad to have you as my
husband. They briefly, smiled at each
other.

Nigel went straight home after he left
the hospital. He called his mom and told
her about his visit with Greg and how
good everything turned out. She was glad
to hear the good report. They only spoke
briefly because Nigel had some things to
take care of. After Nigel ended the
conversation with his mom, he hurried and
finished the things that he needed to get
done for the day. Then, he made a quick
run to the grocery store to get ingredients
for pina coladas and a good meal to go
along with them.

Nigel was going to be entertaining a
young lady that night. It was kind of ironic
because it was Vickie's daughter, Valerie,
the same one that his mom had just told
his dad that she wanted to match him up
with; and Nigel didn't know about what
his mom had said. Nigel and Valerie just

happened to run into each other one day, when Nigel was leaving work to take his lunch break. They saw each other and spoke. They briefly talked and exchanged phone numbers. Nigel promised to call Valerie and have her over at his place for dinner, and he did.

Vickie's daughter, Valerie, was a thick, gorgeous woman, who took good care of herself. She had a beautiful personality and was smart; and Nigel found her very attractive. The feeling was mutual for her. They both possessed the qualities that they each desired, in the person that they were looking for as a companion. They weren't sure how things would turn out if they began a relationship with each other, but they gave it a shot. Nigel's mom was elated when she found out about it. His dad was happy for him, too.

Nigel and Valerie were impressed with each other after their first date; they had dinner and a great time. There was no sex involved during their first date, and they still wanted to see each other, again. When Valerie went to work the next day, after her and Nigel's first date, she was very happy and vibrant. Her co-workers noticed it and inquired about her joviality. Her co-workers' names were Mandy and Patrice. They all worked well together.

Valerie was smart, laid back, and neutral. She wasn't quick to jump on either sides of a debate. She carefully thought things out and tried to make the most sensible decisions. Mandy was laid back, and when there was a debate, she'd always just listen to everyone else's opinion. Then, she'd take the side of the person she felt gave the most reasonable answer. Patrice was silly- the comedian of the office. She just said whatever came to her mind, which was usually radical, and she'd be all over the page.

So, when Valerie told Mandy and Patrice that she was happy because she'd been on her first date with Nigel, they had plenty to say. Mandy said to Valerie, "describe Nigel to us." Valerie replied, "sure, he loves the Lord; he's tall, light skinned, with a slender-muscular build, smart and handsome." "Okay, so he loves the Lord-that's a big plus," said Mandy. "He's also smart, fine, good looking and he's a red bone. Girl, you've got the total package! You know Patrice loves those

CHAPTER NINE
Light skinned vs Dark skinned

red bones. I prefer chocolate, myself; the blacker the berry-the sweeter the juice!" Valerie chuckled. "Ha, ha, ha! Mandy, you're a mess." Mandy said, "hey, I'm just keeping it real."

Valerie replied, "You all need to stop though, with that light skinned versus dark skinned mess. Again, it's about character, not skin color. That's just like the black versus white debate. Some people say that black people steal and are thugs. However, there are also white thieves and thugs; there are thieves and thugs of all races. It's also good people of all races.

Some people say that white people are racist, but there are black folks who are racist, as well.

For instance, when some black men date or marry white women, honey, there are some black women who will get irate about the situation! I know what I'm talking about because I've heard some of them ranting about it. Honestly, I used to feel that way myself. It seemed to me that black men saw black women as being good enough for them, if they didn't have a pot to pee in. However, if they became successful, they'd get with white women, or women of other races. It just seemed that they deserted us black women once they became wealthy, but I had to let that go. It's not good to be like that. I also know a few black, women who are dating white guys; and they're very happy, and that's what matters.

We all need to come together, and love and respect one another. It's bad either way you look at it, when people are hung up on skin color. It's bad when one race thinks they're superior to another because of their skin color, but it's foolish when people of the same race think they're superior because they're of a lighter or darker skin tone. Lord, help us in this world." Valerie shook her head.

Patrice said, "Valerie, we heard everything you said. Now, by the way, what does Nigel's wallet look like? I bet you he's loaded; I'm just saying." "Look you guys, I've told you all many times, that what matters most to me when choosing a companion is if he loves God and has a good character. With that being said, Nigel loves the Lord and he just happens to be good looking, with a corporate job…in that order. Now, I want the both of you to give me your feedback on something that I'm about to ask you all. Okay, just say you've met a guy who is not very good looking, doesn't have a lot of money, but he loves the Lord-would you be okay with that? Mandy, you go first."

"Okay, let me think about this first. Valerie, you said that the fact that a man loves the Lord should matter the most. Well, I do agree with that. As far as the finances and his looks, if I'm working and he works with me, then we can change his financial status. If his finances start to look better, then, I'm sure he'll look better to me, also."

"Ha, ha, ha! Okay, Mandy." Valerie shook her head with a big smile on her face. "What about you, Patrice? What do you think?" "Let me see, here. Um, so basically, you said that he's ugly and broke, but he loves the Lord. Well, I have nothing against a man loving the Lord, but he needs to have something else going for himself. I mean, if he's ugly, but he has money, I may be able to tolerate that-but

ugly and broke?! Nooo, I'm sorry; I
can't...with him. I'm not saying that he
wouldn't be right for someone else. I
believe there would be someone for him-
just not me. Nooo, he can't be broke, and
ugly! Next!!!" "Oh, my goodness, Patrice
you are hilarious-a straight out comedian,
but you've got a lot to learn, sweetie. My
advice hasn't changed; a man's
relationship with God should be the
number one thing that draws you to him.

Now...moving along, you all have
been trying to find out what happened
between Nigel and me. Well, I'll tell you.
He cooked dinner for me and made some
delicious pina coladas. We talked and
laughed. We had lots of fun; and we both
want to see each other, again." Patrice
said, "girl, you mean nothing happened-
like any good, hot, steamy, sex?" "No
Patrice, all that will come in time, if we
get married, one day." Patrice replied,
"girl, please...better you than me. Aint no
way...!" Valerie just shook her head.
"Nope, there was no sex involved and we
both want to continue seeing each other.
How many men you know would've done
that?" Patrice replied, "I don't know any,
and I'm not looking for any like that.

I want somebody who'll blow the cobwebs off at least occasionally." "Now, see, you're a bad role model for other younger girls." "Who? No, I'm not. I'm not saying it's got to be that way for anyone else, but that's how it's got to be for me; that's all. I'm just saying."

"Mandy, you've gotten pretty quiet." "Yeah, I'm just listening, Valerie. I used to think like Patrice, but I became celibate after I accepted the Lord in my life, and I've been living that way ever since. Before I accepted the Lord in my life, guys used to talk about how fine I was; I'd feel good and fall for their lines. I sure was fine…fine and foolish, back then. Now, I believe in waiting until marriage to engage in sex, as well."

Patrice said, "Mandy, gurl, please! Anyhow, how long has it been since you accepted the Lord in your life?" "It's been about 3 years ago now, Patrice." "So, you've been celibate ever since, huh?" "Yep, Patrice, I have…." Patrice shook her head. Valerie said, "okay, you two, I just wanted you all's feedback on that. As far as myself, I know exactly what I'm going to do. I'm going to continue seeing

Nigel, and see where things go from here.
You never know, we may end up wanting
to spend the rest of our lives together.
Should that be the case, then I'll gladly get
my groove on, once we're married, Ms.
Patrice! You ladies are something else, but
I love you both; and if anybody bothers
either one of you, they'll have to come
through me, first. I mean that, too."
Valerie looked at them both and smiled
widely.

Nigel also went to work happy, the
next day after his date with Valerie. A
couple of his male colleagues noticed how
excited he seemed. One of the guys said to
Nigel, "wow! You sure are happy, today.
You're always upbeat, but you're smiling
from ear to ear, today. Isn't he…?" He
asked the other guy. The other guy replied,
"yep" and nodded his head.

Nigel said, "you all know it's been a
while since I've dated anyone. Anyhow, I
had a young lady, Valerie, over last night
for dinner, and I made some delicious pina
coladas. We ate dinner; we talked and
laughed. We had a great time." One of the
guys said, "so, what does she looks like,
man?" "I'll tell you, but first off, she

loves the Lord. Okay, she's a thick woman who takes good care of herself. She's smart, a very sweet young lady, and she's absolutely beautiful. The ironic thing about it is that my mom had wanted to match us up, and I didn't even know it.

We just happened to run into each other while I was out for my lunch break. We spoke and conversed, briefly. Then, we decided to exchange numbers. I told her I'd call her and have her over for dinner; I did that, and I sure am glad that I did because we had an awesome time together. The chemistry between us is amazing. We plan to see each other again, very soon, like this weekend. Ha, ha, ha!"

The guys chuckled with him. One of them said, "I'm glad for you, man." The other guy said, "yeah, I'm happy for you, too, Nigel." "Thanks guys. I'm about to bounce; I'll see you all, later." Nigel left work for that day. He was looking forward to seeing Valerie again, on the coming weekend.

Valerie and Nigel saw each other again that weekend, and they had a great time. She told Nigel about the discussion

CHAPTER TEN
Sex Is Not Love

that she and her co-workers had after finding out that they're dating. "After our first date, the girls at the office were talking about how vibrant and happy I looked. So, I told them that you and I are dating. Of course, they wanted to hear all of the details." "So, what did you tell them?" "I told them that we had a great time together." "Okay, good to know that we share mutual feelings about that. I'm just messing with you, girl." Valerie smiled, also. She would often smile if she simply thought about Nigel.

"I shared with the young ladies at work how that we had dinner and talked…just laughed and enjoyed ourselves. They wanted to know if we had sex. When I told them that we didn't have sex, they seemed surprised. Well, one of them in particular, was surprised. Her name is Patrice. Mandy understands more because she's also a celibate, Christian. She still has some things to learn, though.

Young people have a lot to learn. For one thing, they need to know that **sex is not love.**" "Yeah, they do. I shared with

the guys at work also, about us dating."
"So, how did that go?" "It went well;
they're more of a mature group. They
didn't even go there. One of them inquired
about what you look like." "So, what did
you tell him?" "What did I tell him…what
did I tell him? Ha, ha, ha. I told him that
you love the Lord, and then I told him how
thick and beautiful you are. Was that
okay?" "Yes, of course." "I just wanted
to make sure." Nigel smiled and said,
"after that, they both told me that they
were happy for me; I thanked them, and I
left work and headed home."

Each time Nigel and Valerie went on a
date, they wanted to see each other, again;
and they did. They continued to date one
another although there was never any sex
involved. They started seeing each other
quite often. They grew to love each other,
and they got married at the end of the year.
They had a Christmas wedding. It was
during winter and cold outside, as usual.
However, they had a warm, beautiful,
indoor wedding. Not only did Nigel make
the right choice to forgive, but he made
the right choice in picking the woman that
he took to be his wife.

It can be challenging, sometimes, to have the desire to forgive others. When facing such a challenge, that's the time that we need to go to the Lord in prayer for that situation. He'll give us the strength that we need to forgive others and will show us how to forgive, if we don't know how. Yes, as weird as it may sound to some folks, there are people who don't know how to forgive. However, once they do it, they'll feel so much better. In Matthew 18:21-35, Jesus instructed us to continuously forgive others.

Sometimes, when it comes to the people that have hurt you, you may notice that they have NOT really changed much. You may not care to be around them often, or maybe not at all, which is your choice, if you're in a position whereas you don't have to be around them. Nevertheless, the main thing is that we forgive others.

This is one thing that's for sure, we'll all need forgiveness at some point because we are all made from the dust of the earth. Therefore, we will make mistakes and bad choices sometimes, and the Lord knows this. So, he cautioned us to forgive others because he knows that we'll also need to be forgiven, but to be forgiven ourselves, we must forgive others.

I hope this book will help someone who has been desiring to let go of bitterness and forgive others, but you didn't know where to begin. Open your mouth and/or your mind and confess to God that you forgive them-even if you don't feel like you do at that moment. However, if you're sincere in your heart about it, God will deliver you…freedom will come.

Even as the main character in this book, I can relate to having some real-life experiences with wanting to forgive others for various reasons, but I just didn't know how. I have experienced pain from various situations in my life that one would never imagine judging by the beautiful smile that God has given me. In the past, there came a point when the Lord revealed to me that I had allowed bitterness and unforgiveness to develop in my heart because of things that happened to me. I knew that it was wrong, and I wanted to let go of those things. I would think to myself that I was going to forgive, but I would still feel the pain and bitterness because of my experiences.

However, I didn't know what to do. Then, one day I asked God to give me strength to forgive and to show me how. He spoke to me **something so simple** to do, "to open my mouth and confess to God that I forgive them-even if I didn't feel like I did at that moment." I was sincere in my heart about it. I did it and felt freedom in my spirit.

90

In life, there will be times when people will hurt us. Sometimes, they may do it intentionally and sometimes they may not. However, I'm learning to forgive whether it's intentionally or not. Also, even when I never get an apology, I'm learning to leave it in God's hands. He knows exactly how to work it out.

A note from the Author: My name is Mrs. Raynell White. Rai was my childhood nickname, and even today, people who have known me since then and/or who are close to me still call me Rai. I truly hope that you've enjoyed reading my book. Be sure to check out my other five books, one of which is a children's book. So, if you have young children in your family or know of other young children…be sure to purchase a copy or copies of my children's book, "Japheth Can Count". Blessings to you and yours. Author Rai White

My Other Books

Before And After I Do
Real Love Is….
Real Love Is….2: The 25th Year
Japheth Can Count
From Rags To Stitches

I hope that you'll support me, and I truly hope that you'll enjoy reading my work. Thanks in advance, and Much Love to you.   Author Rai White

This is the fourth novel written by Rai White. She is married, a mother of four young adults, and has one grand baby. She majored in Psychology and has a Degree in Religion. She also has a Certificate for Clinical Pastoral Education (CPE 1), which allowed her the opportunity to work as a Chaplain at an Acute Care Rehabilitation center, which she loved. All her books have a positive message that speaks to the soul.

Beautiful Perspective